Planets

Gail
Tuchman

New ~~~~~~~~~~~~~~~~~~~~~~~~~~~~~~~ d
Sydney Mexico City New Delhi Hong Kong

Read more! Do more!

After you read this book, download your free all-new digital activities.

For Mac and PC

You can show what a great reader you are!

Planet counting

Click on the correct numbers.

DISCOVER MORE! click

BACK TO THE START home

How many ice giants are there?	How many rocky planets are there?	How many planets have rings?	How many planets are tipped on their sides?	How many planets orbit the Sun?
2 3 4	2 4 8	4 6 8	1 2 3	4 6 8

Do quizzes about
the fun facts in this book!

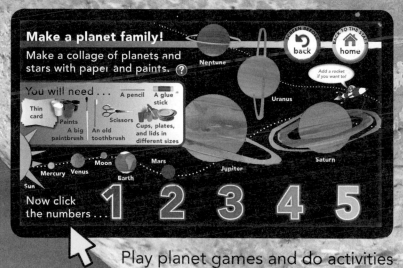

Make a planet family!

Make a collage of planets and
stars with paper and paints. ?

SCREEN BEFORE back

BACK TO THE START home

Add a rocket if you want to!

You will need . . .

Thin card

Paints
A big
paintbrush

An old
toothbrush

A pencil

A glue
stick

Scissors

Cups, plates,
and lids in
different sizes

Neptune

Uranus

Saturn

Sun

Mercury Venus

Moon

Earth

Mars

Jupiter

Now click
the numbers . . .

1 2 3 4 5

Play planet games and do activities
with videos and sounds!

Log on to
**www.scholastic.com/
discovermore/readers**
Enter this special code:
L1DWKNPXN951

What's out there?
Ready? Let's go!

Let's zoom into space.
Let's zoom past
the Moon.

Let's visit the stars and the planets.

Lift off!

5

Most stars have families of planets. The planets in a family orbit, or travel around, the star.

Planets look like balls.

Some stars have only one planet. Some have many.

Star

NEW WORD

orbit

OR-bit

A planet may take a long time to **orbit** a star.

SAY IT OUT LOUD

Our Sun is a star.
Earth orbits the Sun.
Earth is a rocky planet.

One million
Earths could fit
into the Sun!

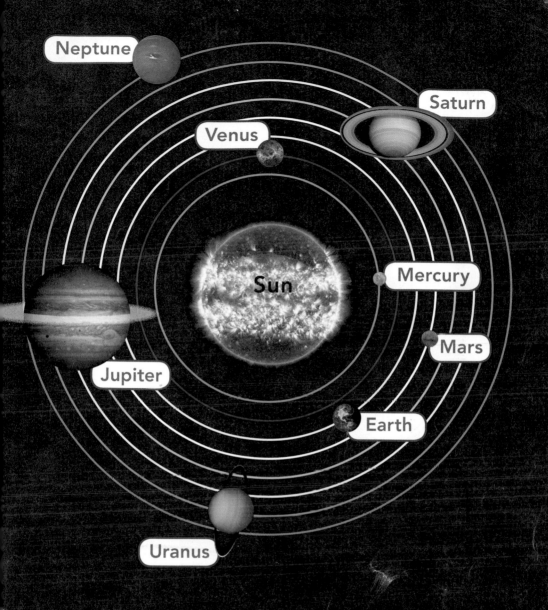

Gas planets and rocky planets orbit our Sun. They are all part of the Sun's family.

Here are the giant gas planets! They are far, far away from the Sun.

Clouds of gas swirl. There's nothing to land on. There's nothing to stand on.

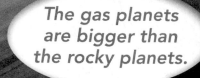

The gas planets are bigger than the rocky planets.

Uranus

Saturn

Neptune

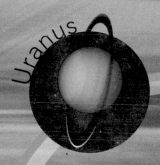

Jupiter

The gas giants have rings spinning around them.

Neptune

Hang on to your space helmet!
Neptune is a windy gas planet.

The gas on
Neptune makes
the planet
look blue!

Neptune has freezing winds.

They blow at more than 1,930 kph!

Gas giant Uranus is tipped on its side. It's the only planet that spins on its side!

WILLIAM AND CAROLINE HERSCHEL

William and Caroline Herschel

This brother and sister worked together more than 200 years ago. They spotted new things in the night sky, including Uranus.

Uranus

Saturn

Saturn is famous for its rings.

Saturn's rings are made of bits of ice and rock.

Gas giant Jupiter does things in a BIG way.

It's the biggest planet in the Sun's family. It also has huge storms. One has been blowing for over 300 years!

Great
Red Spot

The Great Red Spot is a giant storm!

Jupiter

Asteroids rock!
Asteroids ARE rocks!
Most are in the asteroid
belt. This area lies between
Jupiter and Mars.

Ceres is a rocky dwarf planet.

Ceres

The dwarf planet
Ceres is there, too.
A dwarf planet is
a little planet.

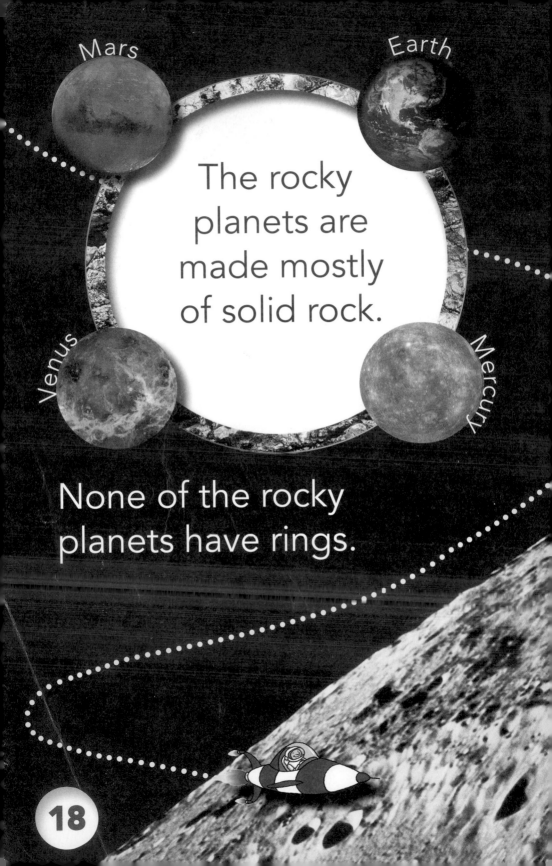

Mars

Earth

Venus

Mercury

The rocky planets are made mostly of solid rock.

None of the rocky planets have rings.

Mars and Earth have moons. Earth has one moon. Mars has two moons.

Earth's Moon

Mars is called the red planet, because it is coated with red dust. It looks red-hot. It is really very, very cold!

Mars

We send robots to Mars to explore!

Earth

Earth has been called the Goldilocks planet.

It is just right for living things!

It is not too hot.

It is not too cold.

It is not too dry.

It is not too wet.

Watch out!

Sun

Venus traps
the Sun's heat.
The planet is
hot, hot, hot!
It SIZZLES.

*The air on Venus
is very thick.*

Venus

Mercury's days are hotter than a pizza oven!

Mercury

Mercury: hot during the day, cold at night.

But its nights are freezing.

23

Meet some other members of our Sun's family.

Haumea   Makemake   Eris

The ice dwarf planets orbit our Sun in the cold space past Neptune.

We are spotting more ice dwarfs every year. There may be hundreds of them!

Pluto

Pluto is the most famous ice dwarf.

Our Sun is one of lots and lots of stars. Other stars have planet families, too. We call these planets exoplanets.

We have found over 1,000 exoplanets!

We sent a telescope to spot exoplanets.

Kepler telescope

Earth

Welcome back to Earth!

Home, sweet home!

What else is out there? We are finding exciting new things every day.

In the coming years,
we'll find out much
more about the planets
in our Sun's family . . .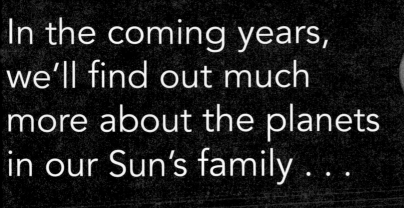

. . . and those far, far away.

Glossary

asteroid
A huge rock that travels around the Sun.

asteroid belt
The area of space between Jupiter and Mars where most asteroids travel around the Sun.

dwarf planet
An object that travels around the Sun that is smaller than a planet.

exoplanet
A planet that travels around a star other than our Sun.

gas giant
A huge planet made mostly of gas.

moon
An object that travels around a planet.

orbit
To travel around a planet or star.

planet
A large, round object that travels around a star.

rocky planet
A planet made mostly of solid rock.

star
A ball of hot, glowing gases.

Sun
The star around which Earth and other planets travel.

Index

For his generosity of time in sharing his expertise, special thanks to Dr Mordecai-Mark Mac Low, Curator, Department of Astrophysics, American Museum of Natural History.

Images
Alamy Images/Mary Evans Picture Library: 13 l; Dreamstime: cover silhouettes (Alder), 21 bl inset (Alphaspirit), 15 br (Andre Adams), 23 r, 24 bg ice, 25 bg ice (B1e2n3i4), 21 bl (Christoph Weihs), 7 b (Dedaiva), 16 asteroid texture, 17 asteroid texture, 18 t bg (Eugenesergeev), 4 fg (Haywiremedia), 21 bg (Iakov Kalinin), 11 inset bg, 24 bg stars, 24 inset bg, 25 bg stars (Igor Sokalski), 21 rcb (Jamen Percy), 6 t, 7 t (Luka137), 6 bg, 7 bg (Mopic), 4 bg, 5 bg (Mpz@sapo.pt), 21 rt, 22 c, 23 l (Nick Anthony), 27 br (Pratik Panda), 21 rb (Roman Sakhno), 2 bg, 3 b bg (Snizhanna), 19 inset (Taichesco), 21 rct (Zastavkin); Ellis Nadler Partnership: cartoon illustrations throughout; Fotolia/clearviewstock: 8 bg; iStockphoto: 9 Earth, 18 Earth, 21 tl (janrysavy), 3 arrow (pagadesign), 2 computer (skodonnell); Media Bakery/Granger Wootz: 5 fg; NASA: 26 inset, 27 bl (Ames/JPL-Caltech), 30, 31 (ESO/L. Calçada/Nick Risinger (skysurvey.org)), 9 Mercury, 18 Mercury, 23 c (Johns Hopkins University Applied Physics Laboratory/Carnegie Institution of Washington), cover fg, 3 t bg, 9 Venus, 18 Venus, 22 b (JPL), 16 main; 17 main (JPL-Caltech), 9 Jupiter, 11 inset br, 15 bg (JPL/University of Arizona), 28 main, 29 (Reto Stöckli, Nazmi El Saleous, and Marit Jentoft-Nilsen, NASA GSFC), 8 fg, 9 sun, 22 t (SDO/AIA/S. Wiessinger), back cover, cover bg, 24 insets, 27 t, 32; Science Source: 14 b, 17 tr (Chris Butler), 10, 11 bg (Detlev van Ravenswaay), 11 inset tr, 24 fg, 25 fg (Friedrich Saurer), 1 (Julian Baum), 26 main (Lynette Cook), 20 b (Millard H. Sharp), 9 Neptune, 11 inset bl, 12 t (Walter Myers), 9 Saturn, 9 Uranus, 9 Mars, 11 inset tl, 13 r, 14 t, 18 bg, 18 Mars, 19 bg, 20 bg, 20 t.